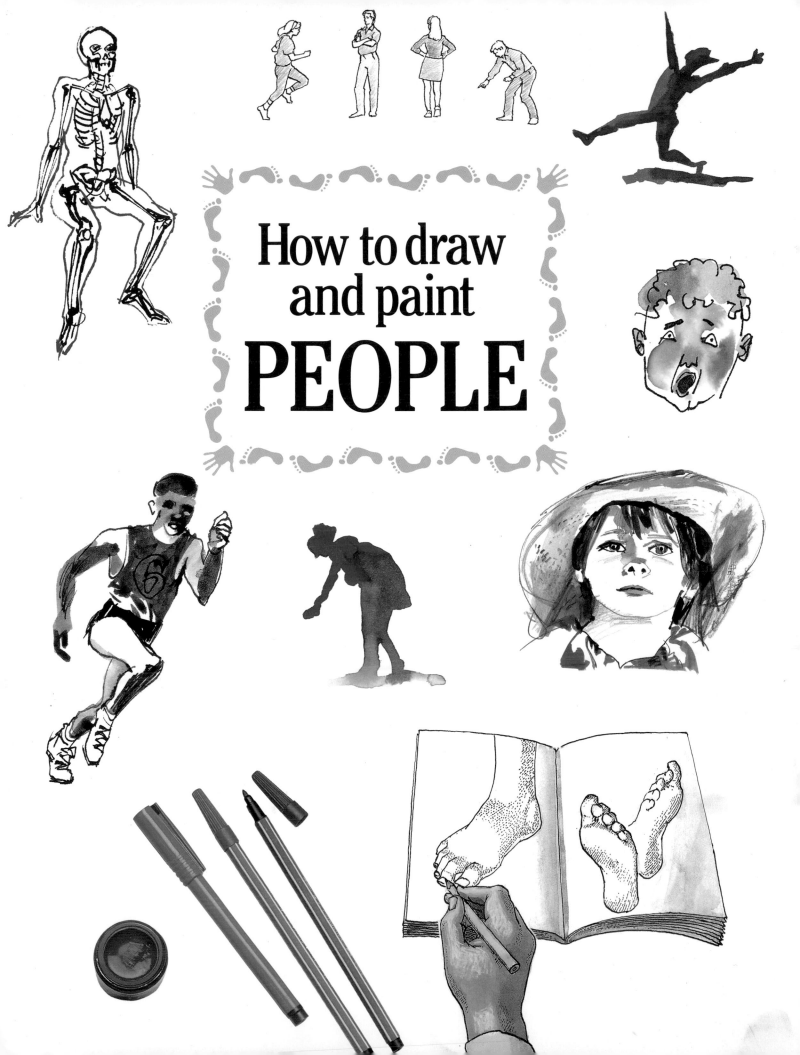

How to draw and paint
PEOPLE

How to draw and paint PEOPLE

ANGELA GAIR

THE APPLE PRESS

A QUARTO BOOK

Published by The Apple Press
6 Blundell Street
London N7 9BH

ISBN 1-85076-353-4

This book was designed and produced by
Quarto Publishing Limited
6 Blundell Street
London N7 9BH

Senior Editor Christine Davis
Editor Sue Baker
Publishing Director Janet Slingsby
Art Director Moira Clinch
Assistant Art Director Chloë Alexander
Designers Hazel Edington, Penny Dawes
Illustrators Kate Gwynn, Sally Launder, Gabriella Baldwin-Purry,
Gay Galsworthy, Cathy May, David Kemp, Moira Clinch, Neal Cobourne
Photographers Paul Forrester, Ian Howes

Acknowledgements
The publishers would like to thank Malcolm Appleby
and the pupils of Warter C.E. Primary School for
their help with the preparation of this book. Thanks also to staff of the
Canonbury Art Shop, London, for their kind co-operation
and loan of materials, and to Sarah Harris and Seth Dawes for
their valuable contribution.

Picture credits: Bridgeman Art Library p12, p66, p71, p75, p86-7;
Tate Gallery, London p88.

Typeset in Great Britain by ABC Typesetters Limited, Bournemouth
Manufactured in Singapore by Chroma Graphics Limited
Printed in Singapore by Kim Hup Lee Printing Co. Pte. Ltd.

Contents

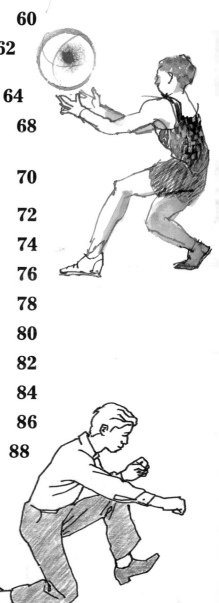

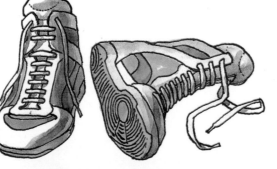

Getting started

A nyone can paint and draw people – it is just a matter of developing the talent. It is like learning to play football, or tennis, or a musical instrument – practise every day and you will find you get better and better. This book will give you lots of ideas to try out at home or at school.

There are all sorts of different paints, papers and drawing materials in the shops. It is important to choose the right materials for each kind of artwork. They are described in later chapters – but here are some items you will need when you start painting and drawing.

Brushes

It is important to have good paint brushes. The ones that come in most painting sets aren't very good – they are too floppy and the hairs fall out. Ask for brushes made of hog's hair or nylon. They are not too expensive and they last a long time. You will need a small watercolour brush that comes to a point, for painting small details; also a large brush with a longer handle for painting big shapes.

Paper

There are several kinds of paper, and it comes in a variety of colours. You can buy paper in sheets or in pads. *Sugar paper* is fine if you are using powder paints, pastels or crayons. *Cartridge paper* has a nice surface for pencil drawing. You can buy special paper for painting in watercolour. Because it is white, it makes your paint colours really sparkle. It is also a good idea to buy a small sketching pad which you can carry around with you.

Paint palettes

You can buy special paint palettes for mixing your paints, but old dishes and plates do just as well – the bigger the better, so you have plenty of room to mix your colours.

Drawing board

You will need a hard surface to support your paper when you draw and paint. You can buy one ready-made, or make one from chipboard or plywood. Use clips or drawing pins to attach the paper to the board.

Tips

So you've bought your paint, papers and brushes and you're ready to paint a masterpiece! Here are some tips to help you get started.

- **Keep it clean** Wear old clothes when you are painting, or borrow an old shirt to protect your clothes from paint splashes.

- **Get organized** Make sure you have everything you need *before* you start.

- **Prevent accidents** Give yourself as much room as possible; it will stop you spilling water jars or knocking things onto the

floor. If you are right-handed keep your paints and water jar on your right side, or the other way round

if you are left-handed. This stops you dripping paint on your paper when you reach over to dip your brush.

- **Save it** Save money, and help protect the environment by re-using materials that normally get thrown away. For instance, save old jars, dinner plates and plastic pots for mixing paints. (Liquid detergent bottles with the tops cut off are useful too.) Cut up old clothes to make rags for mopping up. Collect newspapers for protecting your work table (and the floor!) Save small objects like bottle tops, buttons, dried pasta shapes and shiny sweet wrappers for when you make collage pictures. Use scrap paper for testing pencils, brushes and paint mixes.

7

Drawing heads

Before you learn how to draw the different features of the face – the eyes, ears, nose and mouth – you first need to know how to draw heads, and how to find the correct position to place the features on the face. It is difficult to know where to begin. Sometimes we make the nose too long, or place the eyes too high up on the face. Sometimes we put the mouth too low, or the ears in the wrong place. Here are some tips that will help you avoid making mistakes.

How the head sits on the neck
When you draw a figure, be careful not to draw the neck too thin.
The drawing on the right is correct.
The neck is nearly as wide as the face (check this for yourself by looking in the mirror!)

How to draw a head
Seen from the front, the
head is shaped like an egg,
with the pointed end down.

Start by drawing the
shape of the head. Then
draw a line down the
middle of the head. This
gives you the position for
the nose and the centre of
the mouth.

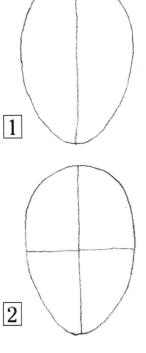

1

The hairline is about one-
third down from the top of
the head to the eyes.

Draw a line across the
middle of the head. This is
where the eyes are
positioned.

2

The eyes are halfway down
the head.

The ears line up between
the eyebrows and the tip of
the nose.

The tip of the nose is
halfway between the
eyebrows and the bottom
of the chin.

The lower lip is halfway
between the tip of the nose
and the bottom of the chin.

Draw another line
halfway below that. This is
where the tip of the nose
will come. Draw another
line halfway between the
nose line and the bottom of
the chin. This is where the
mouth will go. Now you
can draw in the eyes, nose
and mouth in their correct
positions. The ears line up
between the eyebrows and
the tip of the nose.

3

Egg-heads

We don't always see people's faces
from straight in front. When someone
is looking up, down, or to one side,
their head is tilted at an angle – and
this makes the features even more
difficult to draw! You can make a
simple model that will help you to see
what happens to the features of the
face when the head is tilted at
different angles.

Take a hard-boiled
egg and hold it
pointed end down.
Using the measuring
method above, draw
eyes and a mouth on

the egg. Make a nose
out of plasticine and
stick it on the egg.
Tip the "egg-head"
forwards, backwards
and to either side.

Make drawings of
your egg-head
model from different
angles.

Eyes

When we look at a person we usually notice their eyes first. The eyes are the most expressive feature of the face – they can tell us a lot about a person's feelings.

Eyes differ in shape, size and colour from one person to another. But everyone's eyes are made in the same way. You will find it easier to draw and paint eyes if you understand how they are formed. Let's take a closer look at eyes.

Right: Eye shapes vary a lot. Look how the upper and lower eyelids curve on each eye – for example, the bottom lid on the top eye is almost flat but its top lid is much more curved.

The middle eye's curves are almost identical. Look at the eye corners – in the top and bottom eyes they are level with each other, but on the middle eye they are on a slope.

Below: It helps to understand how eyes fit into the skull in order to draw them. You only see part of an eyeball – the rest is hidden behind the eyelids. Use your fingertip

to feel the roundness of your eyeballs through your upper eyelids.

With what you know about eye shapes, you can start drawing them in step-by-step stages.

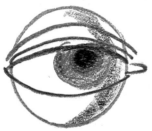

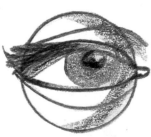

1 To draw an eye from the front, draw a circle for the eyeball. Add eyelids, with the corners on the ball sides.

2 Outline the pupil and add a line to show the eyelid thickness. Shade the dark side of the eyeball.

3 Colour the iris; add a small loop on the right corner for the tear duct. A rough line shows the eyebrow.

4 Add eyelashes to complete the eye. Highlights on the iris and pupil will make the eye look really round and shiny.

1 The opening of an eye seen from the side looks like a slice of cake, with its corner in the eyeball centre.

2 Add shading to one side of your eyeball to give it real shape and a feeling of solidity.

3 When you draw the iris and the pupil you will not be able to see all of them – they should be oval shaped.

4 Finish off the eye with some eyelashes – don't forget that upper eyelashes are longer than lower ones.

The distance between eyes varies slightly from person to person. Usually, however, you'll find the distance between the two inner eye corners is about one eye width, as shown right.

Your eyes are a dead giveaway when it comes to showing your emotions! Without looking at the captions to the pairs of eyes below, see if you can tell what sort of emotion each pair of eyes is showing.

This person's eyes have been crying – the edges of the eyelids are red and there are shiny highlights on the lower eyelids.

This pair of eyes suggest someone smiling. The eyes look straight forward and there are wrinkles – "laughter lines" – around the eyes.

This person looks worried and thoughtful – perhaps he's wondering how he did in an exam!

If you are scared of spiders, this is how you'd look if you saw one on your wrist!

You can't believe what you're hearing, and your eyes are wide open in astonishment!

People who are angry screw their eyelids together – the closer they are, the angrier the expression.

This portrait of a woman is by Frans Hals, a Dutch artist of the seventeenth century. Look at the way he has captured the model's expression. Remember that when you smile, you smile not only with your lips but also with your whole face. Cover up the mouth in the painting and you will see that the woman's eyes are smiling, too. When you go to an art gallery, look carefully for the expressions in people's eyes in different pictures.

Look at the difference between the eyes in these three pictures. Babies have big eyes, old people have wrinkly eyes. When you draw or paint someone, make sure you look at the eyes very carefully; they can make a lot of difference to a picture!

Some common mistakes

 Here the eyes have been put too high up on the head.

✓ The eyes should be positioned about half way down the head.

✗ Putting the iris in the middle of the eye makes your model look like a zombie!

✓ Remember that part of the iris is covered by the upper eyelid.

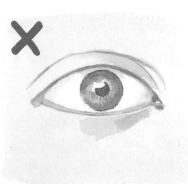

Mouths

T he mouth is a very expressive part of the face. A smiling mouth tells us that someone is happy, but lips that are tight and thin tell us that someone is angry. When you paint or draw a portrait, pay special attention to the mouth because its shape and expression are part of the character of the face. Here are some useful tips to help you to draw and paint mouths realistically.

The lips are not flat and straight but follow the curve of the teeth. Imagine the face as a cylinder – like a tin of baked beans!

When the face is turned a little to one side, you can see the curved shape of the mouth more clearly.

When a person laughs, you can see clearly how the lips are drawn back over the curve of the teeth.

You can show the curved shape of the lips in your paintings and drawings by using the contrast of light and shade. This mouth looks flat because it has been painted all one colour.

This mouth looks more realistic because the artist used a darker shade for the shadowed parts of the lips and a lighter shade for the parts that stick out and catch the light.

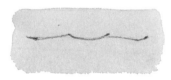

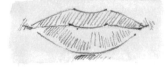

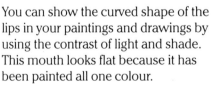

How to draw the mouth
1 Start by drawing the dark line between the lips.

2 Very lightly draw the outline of the upper and lower lips.

3 Look carefully for the patches of light and shadow on the lips. Start by shading in the lightest parts, using very light pencil strokes.

4 Add more pencil strokes to shade in the dark areas. Don't forget the tiny shadow underneath the bottom lip.

14

The mouth from the front

Notice how some parts of the lips look paler than others, where the light hits them.

The top lip is usually thinner and a little longer than the bottom lip.

The line between the lips is the darkest part. Often there is a shadow just underneath this line.

There is a small shadow under the bottom lip.

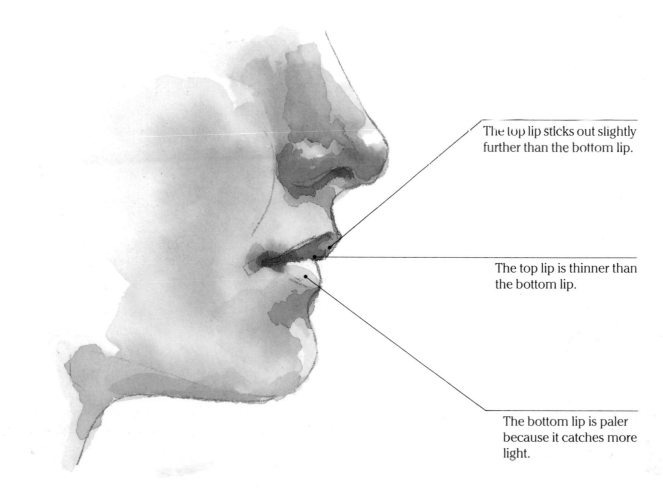

The mouth from the side

The top lip sticks out slightly further than the bottom lip.

The top lip is thinner than the bottom lip.

The bottom lip is paler because it catches more light.

Babies and small children have small mouths, with plump and full lips.

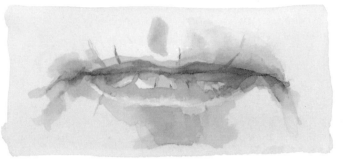

As people get older, they develop wrinkles around their mouths.

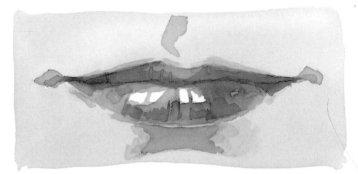

Men's lips are usually longer and narrower than women's lips.

Women tend to have shorter but fuller lips than men's lips.

Laughing lips

Even without the rest of a face, the mouth can tell you what a person is feeling. This picture by the French artist Toulouse Lautrec, painted in 1899, shows a woman who is obviously happy, enjoying jokes with friends at dinner. More than anything else, her mouth and lips show enjoyment.

The close-up below shows how the artist used bright red paint for the lips, and gave them an exaggerated shape, to draw our attention to them.

There are lots of different ways to draw mouths, though. Compare this picture with the *Mona Lisa* opposite.

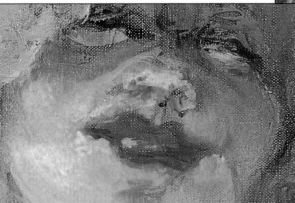

You will probably recognize this painting. It is the *Mona Lisa* by Leonardo da Vinci. It is probably the most famous painting in the world. It was painted hundreds of years ago (in 1507). Today it hangs in the Louvre in Paris, and every year thousands of people come to marvel at the mysterious, bewitching smile of the Mona Lisa.

Noses and ears

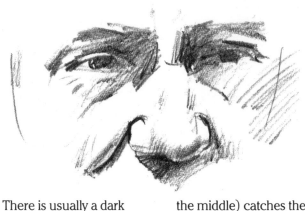

When you draw noses, look carefully at the areas of light and shadow that reveal their form. Leave the light parts white and shade in the shadowed parts. This is how artists show how the nose sticks out from the face – without light and shade the nose would look flat. (Turn to page 48 if you want to learn more about light and shade.)

Drawing a nose from the front

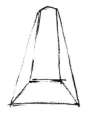

1 The middle section is a wedge shape.

2 The tip is ball-shaped.

3 The nostrils are wing-shaped.

Drawing a nose from the side

1 The basic shape is a triangle.

2 The tip is ball-shaped.

3 The nostril is wing-shaped.

There is usually a dark shadow beneath the nose, and another shadow down one side. The bridge of the nose (the bony part down the middle) catches the light, and so does the soft tip of the nose. The nostrils are the darkest parts.

When you have the shape right, rub out the guide lines or draw on top of them and fill in the areas of light and shade with pencil strokes.

Look at people in a queue, or at the supermarket check-out. You'll see an amazing variety of ears and noses!

18

Ears

You can draw friends' ears while they watch television or chat. Draw the ears from the front (some people's ears stick out more than others'!) Then move round to one side of your model and draw the ear from full view. This is more difficult, because the ear is such a funny shape. When you look into the ear you can see the strange, uncurling forms, as if it was searching for sound. Don't worry if your first drawings are not very good. Keep practising and you will get better and better!

This drawing shows the position of the ear on the side of the head. It lines up with the eyebrow at the top and the tip of the nose at the bottom. Its position is in the middle of the head – further away from the face than you might think.

Drawing an ear

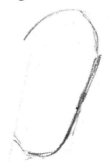 

1 Draw the outline of the ear first.

2 Draw the earhole.

3 Fit the spiralling shapes in between.

4 Look for the shadows inside the ear and shade them in.

From the front, the ear is a squashed-up shape. Look for the contrast between light and shadow.

19

"Identikit" faces

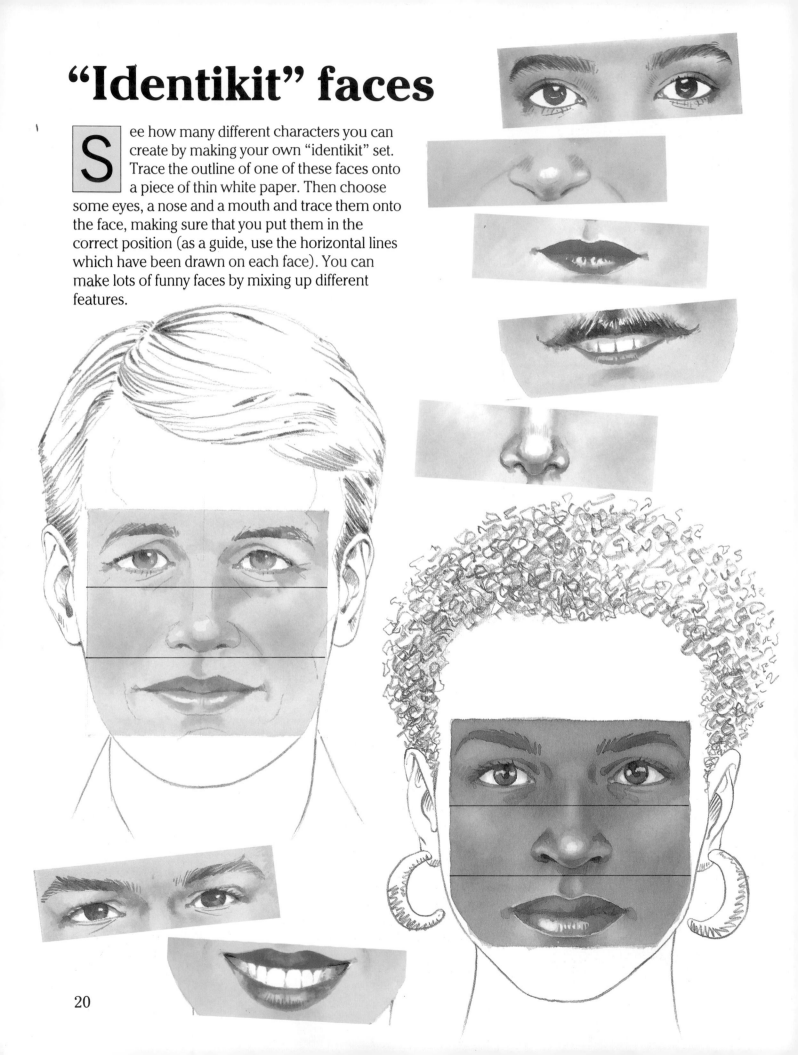

See how many different characters you can create by making your own "identikit" set. Trace the outline of one of these faces onto a piece of thin white paper. Then choose some eyes, a nose and a mouth and trace them onto the face, making sure that you put them in the correct position (as a guide, use the horizontal lines which have been drawn on each face). You can make lots of funny faces by mixing up different features.

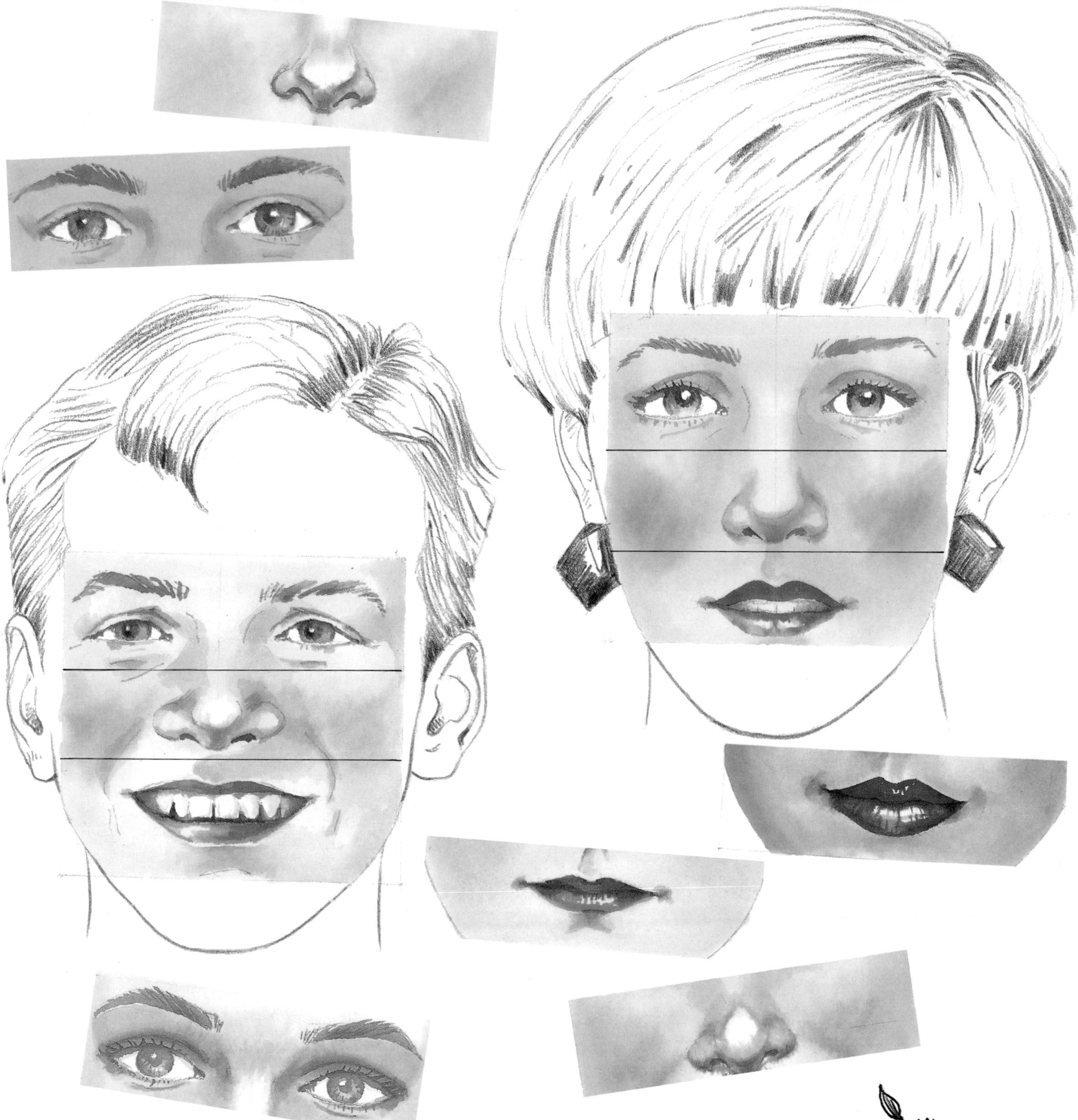

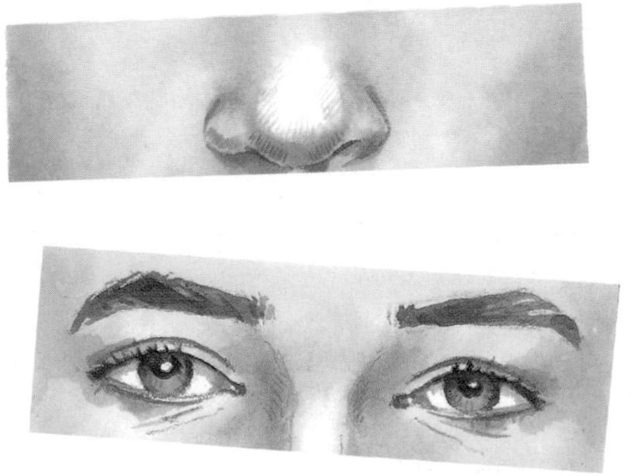

Arty says...
To make your identikit
picture more interesting,
draw and cut out your own
"extras" – beards,
moustaches, hats,
earrings, different
hairstyles and so on. Cut
out faces from magazines
and newspapers and use
them as reference.

Cartoon time

Everyone loves cartoons. Popeye, Charlie Brown and TinTin are just some of our favourite human cartoon characters. Why not try making cartoon drawings of your friends and family? Or find a newspaper picture of a famous person and make a cartoon "portrait" of him or her. You can also have fun making up your own imaginary cartoon character. Or draw cartoon faces with different expressions – happy, sad, angry or frightened. You will get lots of ideas by looking at cartoons in books and newspapers, and by observing people around you.

To create a funny cartoon figure, pick out one or two obvious features, such as a large nose or an unusual hairstyle and exaggerate them – in a friendly way, of course! Here are some ideas to get you started . . .

Look at the different expressions you can capture with just a line for a mouth and dots for eyes.

A downward mouth and screwed up eyes show an angry person.

Miss Prim. The cartoonist has given her a long face and no chin, spectacles, a funny hairdo, a pointed nose and a prim little mouth.

An upward mouth and raised eyebrows show a happy person.

Here's the retired colonel, still barking out his orders. See how his open mouth is exaggerated.

Cartoon children usually have freckles, big ears and messy hair!

Exaggerate people's shapes for a humorous effect. In cartoons, tall, thin people have stretched out heads and necks and long, skinny arms and legs. Short, fat people have round heads and no neck, short legs and big tummies.

Aaagh! Someone has just seen a ghost. A wide open mouth, saucer eyes and hair standing on end express fear – yet the face is still funny.

Measuring the body

When you draw or paint a picture of someone, do you sometimes find that you have made the head too big, or the legs too short, or the hands too small? If you want your pictures of people to look realistic, you have to get all the different parts of the body in correct *proportion*. At first you may think this is very hard – no two bodies are exactly the same. What's more, the younger someone is, the bigger the head is in relation to the rest of the body. Luckily, whether a person is young or old, short or tall, or fat or thin, there are some simple rules to help you get different parts of the body looking right and in proportion to each other.

In babies the head goes about 4 times into the height of the body.

In older children the head goes about 6 times into the height of the body.

When the arms are stretched out, the length from the fingertips of one hand to the fingertips of the other hand is equal to the height of the body.

In adults the head goes about 7 times into the height of the body.

The elbow comes about halfway down the arm.

The legs start about halfway down the body.

When the arms hang at the sides, the tips of the fingers reach down to halfway between the hips and the knees.

The knees are about halfway down the legs.

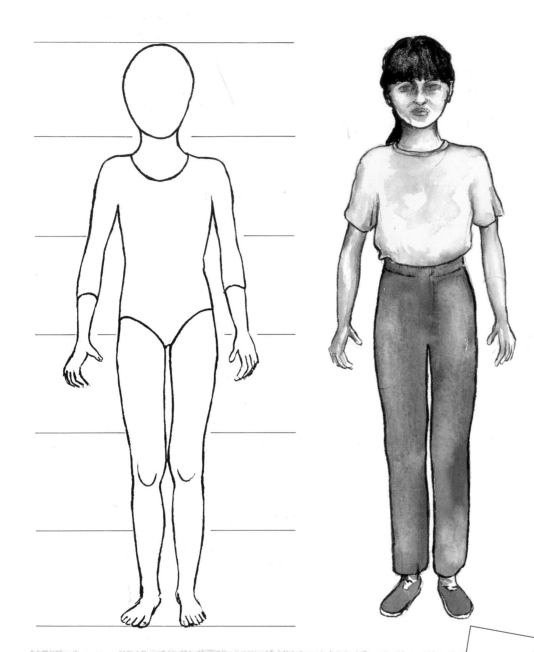

When you draw a figure start by drawing an oval shape for the head. Measure the head length from top to chin and mark off this length 5 more times if you are drawing a child, or 6 more times if you are drawing an adult. Draw these marks lightly so you can rub them out later.

Heads you win!

The head-measuring method is a good way to check that your drawing will fit on the page. If you don't measure, you might reach the bottom of the page before you finish your drawing. Seth, aged 11, drew these two pictures. Guess which one used the "head-measuring" method!

The human body comes in all sorts of sizes and shapes. Just look around you – some people are fat, some are tall and skinny, some are short. Everybody looks different, but the proportions of the body are nearly always about the same.

Drawing the body

The human body is made up of many complicated shapes so it is easier to draw if you start with soft pencil guidelines, breaking it down into simple shapes first. Think of the body as being made up of bits of scrap – rather like the Tin Man from the film *The Wizard of Oz*. The head is shaped like an egg, the arms and legs like sausages, and so on. Following the steps below, you can make your own "Tin Man". When you have completed your "Tin Man" drawing you can start to build up the body in more detail to make it more realistic.

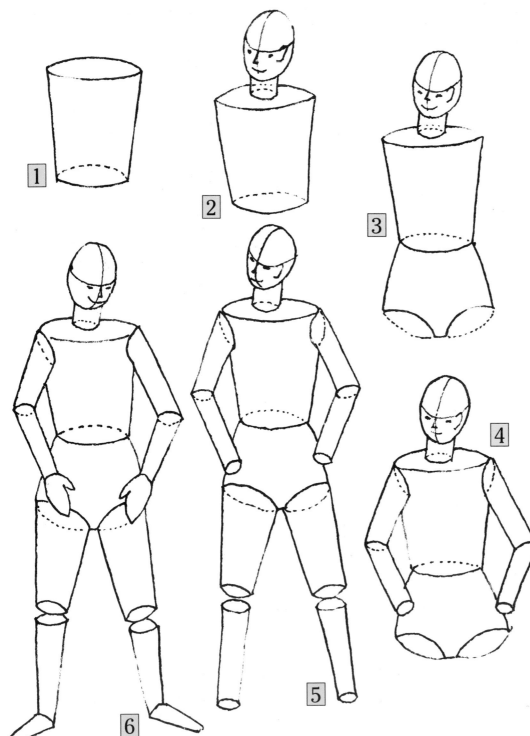

1 The chest is shaped like a bucket.

2 Add on an egg shape for the head and a tin can for the neck.

3 The tummy and hips are shaped like a pair of shorts.

4 The arms are like sausages joined in the middle.

5 The tops of the legs are like cardboard rolls, fatter at the top than at the bottom. The bottoms of the legs are the same, but thinner.

6 Add on simple mitten shapes for the hands and wedge shapes for the feet.

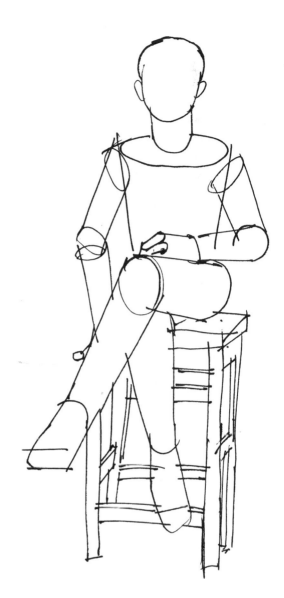

The "Tin Man" method works especially well when you are drawing people in complicated poses. It helps you to see the positions of the limbs more clearly.

Using the simple drawing as a guide, you can now start to draw your model's clothes. The artist has done this in the picture on the right.

When the drawing is finished, rub out the guidelines.

Now try drawing some "Tin Men" of your own in lots of different poses.

29

People moving

Drawing people who are moving may seem difficult at first. But it's like learning to ride a bike – the more you practise the easier it becomes. And moving figures can make your pictures really exciting!

Before starting to draw a moving figure, spend some time just sitting and watching. Concentrate all your attention on the action of the figure, and how the legs, arms, head and back are positioned. Notice how the balance of the body changes during the action. Perform the action yourself if it helps. Now have a go at a lot of quick sketches. Don't worry about mistakes – the important thing is to catch the shape and expression of the body.

Nikki, aged 8, made this chalk drawing of a runner. He looks as if he is going to sprint right off the page!

When you draw figures in action, try drawing sweeping lines that follow the direction of the motion.

This will help you to convey a feeling of speed and movement, and make your figures seem more realistic.

30

Make a flick book

To make a flick book you will need a small notebook and a pen or pencil. The idea is to make small sketches of a moving figure on the corners of the pages, then flick the pages very fast to make the figure "move".

Make your first sketch in the bottom corner of the last page – not the first page – of your notebook. Make your second sketch in the bottom corner of the page before that, and so on until the movement is completed.

Lift up the pages at the corner with your thumb and rapidly flick them. As you do this, your figure will appear to "walk". This is similar to the way in which cartoon films are made.

Get a friend to repeat a simple movement such as walking. At several points during the action ask him or her to stop and hold the pose while you make quick "pin man" sketches.

Sports grounds and dance classes are good places to go to draw moving figures. Dancers and sports players repeat the same actions again and again. This makes it easier to record the movements.

31

Scribble drawing

Take your sketchbook along to a sports centre or ice rink and make lots of speedy scribble drawings of figures in action. Try to catch the actions and poses with just two or three strokes of your pencil. The drawings don't have to be accurate. You are not drawing the people, but what they are *doing*.

Use your whole arm as you draw, not just your fingers and wrist, and make fast, loose strokes. Keep your pencil moving all the time, hardly ever lifting it from the paper. Can you see how the scribbled lines give a feeling of movement to the figures?

These "scribble drawings" were made at a football match. When you have a go at "scribble drawing", why not try drawing without looking at the paper. This can help you to look carefully at the person you're drawing – and you might be surprised at the results!

32

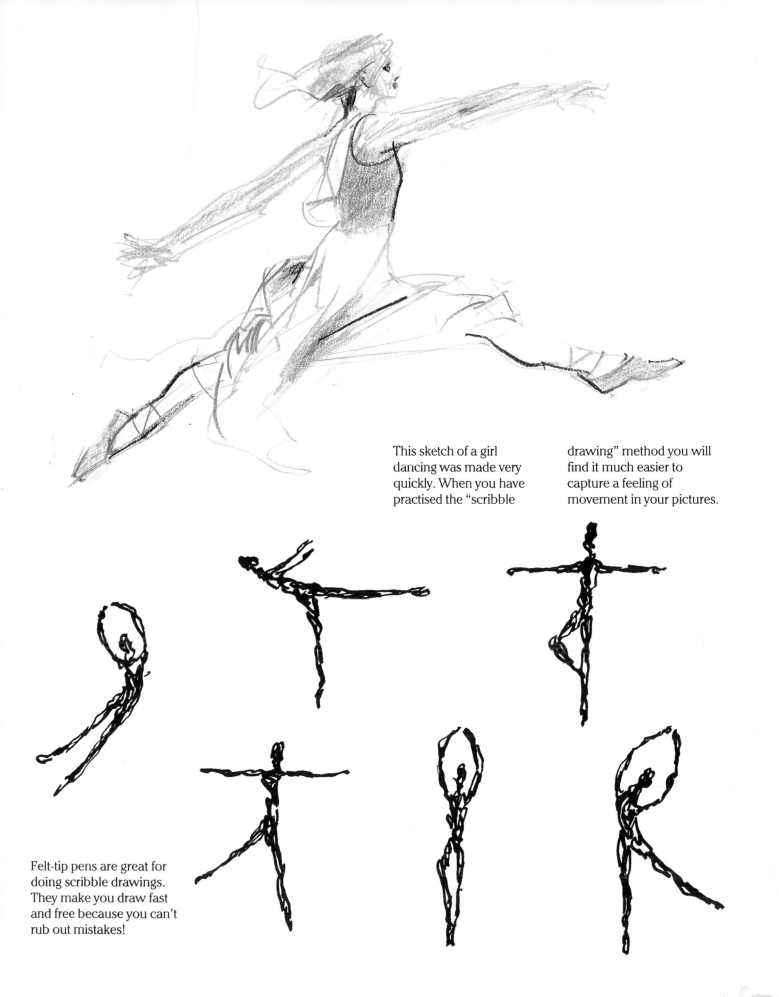

This sketch of a girl dancing was made very quickly. When you have practised the "scribble drawing" method you will find it much easier to capture a feeling of movement in your pictures.

Felt-tip pens are great for doing scribble drawings. They make you draw fast and free because you can't rub out mistakes!

Expressions

You know what sort of mood someone is in by the expression on their face. Every day you will see all sorts of expressions – happy, sad, excited, bored, angry, surprised or afraid. The best way to learn to draw expressions is by making faces in a mirror and watching how your mouth, eyes, eyebrows and cheeks change shape as you change expression.

When you are worried your face looks long. Your mouth and eyes droop and look sad.

Here's an angry face. This man looks like a snarling dog!

This is a jealous face. The mouth and eyes are mean.

When you laugh the corners of your mouth turn up.

When you are afraid your mouth goes small and tight and your eyes widen.

When you are surprised your mouth drops open, your eyes open wide and your eyebrows shoot up.

Pulling faces

Look at these six different faces. Can you describe the feeling each one expresses? Choose two different faces and see if you can copy them. Use pencils, paints or crayons. Both the eyes and the mouth show a person's mood. Cover up the eyes on each photo – you can still tell the person's mood by looking at the mouth.

Body language

It is not just the face that expresses someone's mood or personality – so does the body. When people are happy or excited they jump around and wave their arms in the air. When they are angry they may stand with legs apart, head thrust forward and hands on hips. When they are sad their head is bowed and their shoulders droop. Body and face expressions make your paintings of people come to life.

35

Hands up!

Hands are bigger than you might think. Look in a mirror and hold your hand up in front of your face, with your wrist resting on your chin. You will see that from the wrist to the fingertips your hand is almost as long as your face and about half as wide.

Hands seem difficult to draw at first because they are a funny shape. Three main shapes make up the hand. These are the thumb, the fingers and the palm area. Begin by drawing these sections as simple shapes, as shown on the right. Once you have drawn these simple shapes, you can start to add more details and shading to make them look more real.

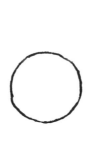

1 Start with a circle for the palm.

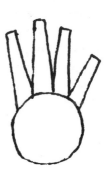

2 Add on the fingers (notice that the middle finger is the longest).

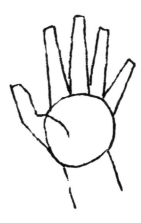

3 Add on the thumb. It is much shorter than the other fingers.

4 Now draw the hand and finger shapes properly and rub out your pencil guidelines.

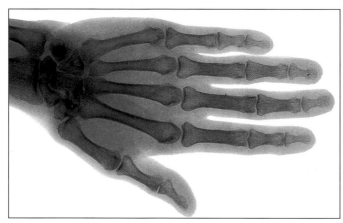

This X-ray picture shows the bone structure of the hand. The finger bones fan out from the wrist.

Draw your own hand

Place your hand, with the fingers spread, on a sheet of paper and draw around it. Then take your hand away and draw in the nails and knuckles.

You can also make hand prints by pressing your hand into a dish of face paint or poster paint and then pressing it onto a sheet of paper.

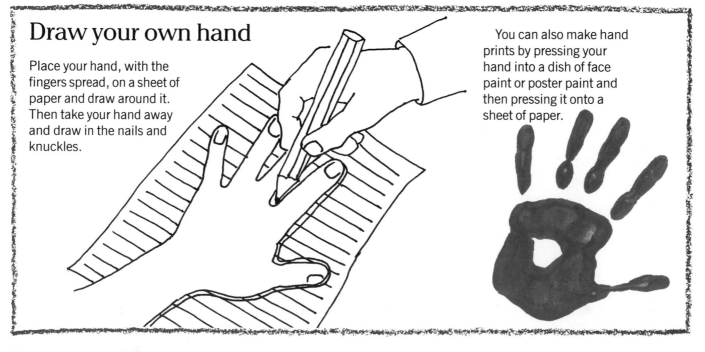

Ask your friends or family to keep their hands still for you while they are reading or watching TV. Draw as many different hands as you can – men's hands, women's hands, old hands, young hands, and so on. Or practise drawing your own hand, stretched out or clenched into a fist. After some practice see if you can draw hands holding a book, or sewing.

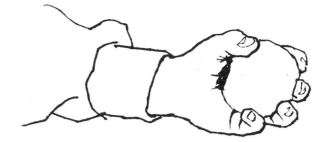

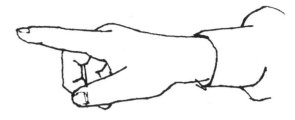

The fingers taper towards the ends, but widen out at the joints.

The fingers are about half the length of the whole hand.

Look at the shapes in between the fingers – it helps you to get the shapes of the fingers right.

The width across the knuckles is about the same as the length of the fingers.

The fingers have two joints but the thumb only has one.

Feet First

We don't take much notice of our feet, probably because they are usually hidden inside shoes and socks. But when you draw and paint people, it is important to know how to draw both bare feet and feet wearing shoes.

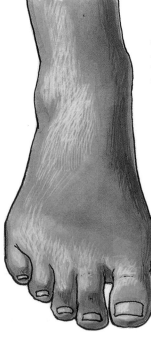

Make drawings of your friends' feet, from different angles. Try to fill the whole page with one drawing.

A foot seen from the side

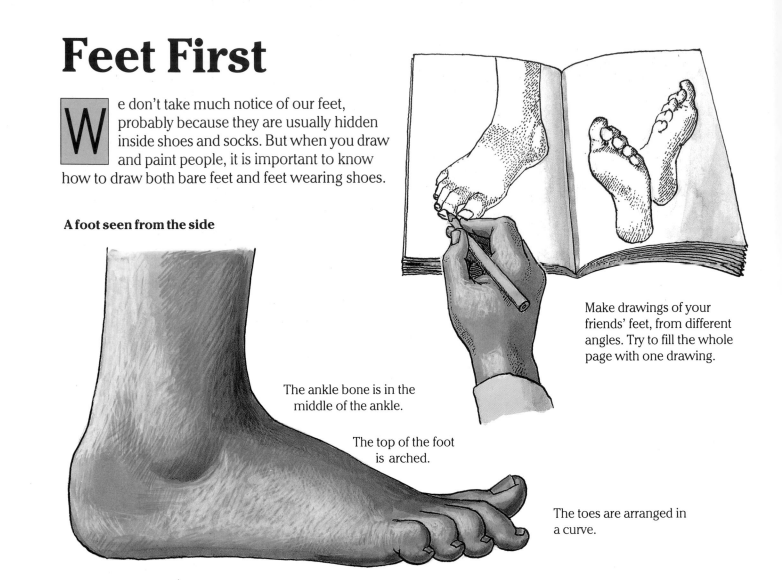

The ankle bone is in the middle of the ankle.

The top of the foot is arched.

The toes are arranged in a curve.

A foot seen from the front

The inside ankle bone is higher than the outside ankle bone.

The foot looks shorter than it does when we see it from the side.

The big toe has only one joint. The others have two.

The ends of the toes have rounded pads.

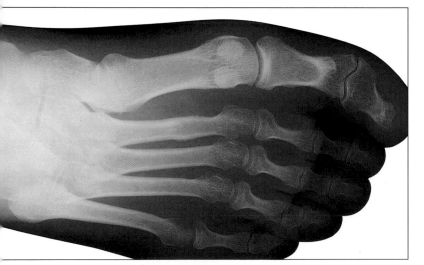

This X-ray picture of a foot shows how many small bones it contains.

Shoes come in all shapes and sizes. Here are just a few. How many other kinds can you think of?

Foot prints

If you look at the soles of wellies, boots and sports shoes, you will see that they have interesting raised patterns, called tread patterns. You can use these patterns to make prints.

Get a friend to wear a pair of boots or sports shoes and stand on a sheet of card or stiff paper. Draw around the edge of the shoes, then cut out the shapes.

Using pieces of scrap such as corrugated card, string, cork or plastic foam, copy the shapes of the raised patterns on the soles. Glue these onto the card sole shapes.

Brush the raised patterns with poster paint and make prints on paper. See how many different patterns you can collect.

Pencils

A pencil and a sheet of paper are all you need to start drawing. Artists like to have plenty of pencils, which they use for making quick sketches as well as detailed drawings. Pencils are great "thinking sticks". With a pencil in your hand, you can put down on paper all those brilliant ideas you have in your head!

Take a large piece of paper and try doing some doodles with your pencils. Draw circles, squiggles, straight lines and criss-cross lines. Press hard with the pencil, then press lightly. Try out different kinds of paper, too: some papers, such as brown parcel paper, have interesting textures that show through when you rub over them with the side of the pencil.

Arty says...
When you draw, hold your pencil further away from the point than you do when you are writing. This will give you more freedom of movement.

Try drawing lines at different speeds. Make fast, zig-zag lines, slow, wavy lines and so on. Do you see how these lines create different feelings?

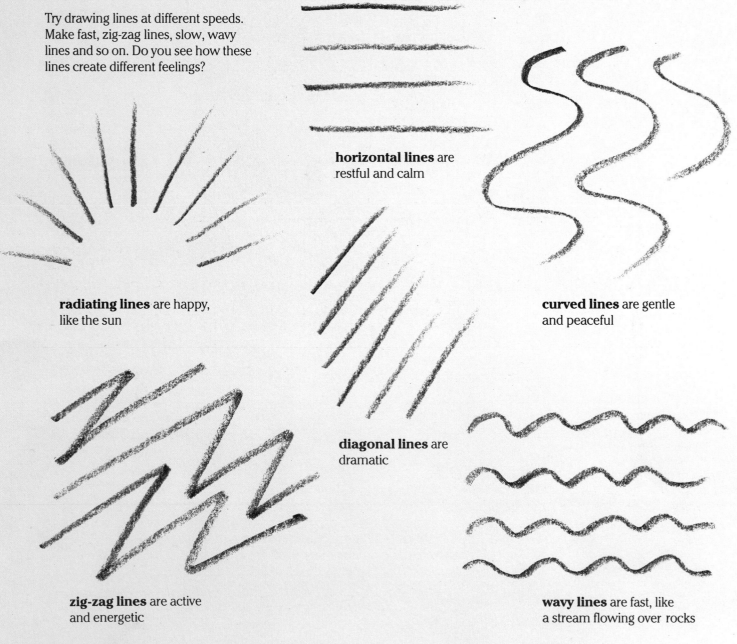

radiating lines are happy, like the sun

horizontal lines are restful and calm

curved lines are gentle and peaceful

diagonal lines are dramatic

zig-zag lines are active and energetic

wavy lines are fast, like a stream flowing over rocks

40

Make a copy of this drawing and try out the different methods the artist used.

Use the pencil point to draw dots and dashes.

Diagonal lines that criss-cross each other make interesting patterns. You can draw the lines close together or far apart.

These soft marks are made by rubbing with the side of a soft pencil. Smudge the marks with your fingertip to make them even softer.

Lots of diagonal lines drawn close together are called "hatching". This is good for shading.

Pencil leads come in different grades, from very hard to very soft. Hard pencils range from H to 12H (the hardest). Soft pencils range from B to 8B (the softest). HB and F are in between.

Soft pencils make broad, dark lines. They are also good for shading.

Hard pencils make thin, light lines. They are good for drawing details and patterns.

Erasers can be used for smudging pencil lines together as well as for rubbing out mistakes.

41

Pastels and coloured pencils

Pastels and coloured pencils are good for sketching outdoors because they are easy to carry and you don't need brushes and water to mix the colours.

Pastels are made from coloured powder mixed with gum and rolled into sticks. There are hundreds of wonderful colours to choose from but it is best to start off with just a few, or buy a boxed set. Pastels are soft and crumbly, so you can blend colours together on your paper by rubbing them with your fingertip. Use the point to make sharp lines. Snap a piece off the stick and use it on its side to colour in large areas. Pastel smudges easily, so keep your hand above the paper as you draw, and keep blowing away the dust.

Oil pastels are similar to ordinary pastels, but the colours are stronger. Oil pastels don't smudge.

Coloured pencils also come in dozens of different colours, and you can buy sets in boxes. Their sharp points are good for drawing small details. You can also buy special watercolour pencils. With these you can draw and paint at the same time! You draw with the pencil in the normal way, then brush over the lines with a brush and water. The colour dissolves and you can spread it with your brush, just like paint.

This picture of a girl flying a kite was made with pastels and coloured pencils. Try experimenting with the different effects you can get using a mixture of techniques.

A sharp-pointed pencil was used for this line.

Thick white pastel has been used here to give the effect of sunlight falling on the girl's dress.

Here colours have been blended together on the paper by rubbing with the fingertip.

To colour in the ground area, the artist held the pastel on its side and rubbed it across the page.

Drawing yourself

I f you want to learn more about drawing portraits, a good way is to set up a mirror and draw yourself. As you don't have to ask someone else to pose for you, you can work on your drawing any time you like.

A dressing table mirror is useful because you can rest your drawing board on the edge of the table and the mirror is just the right distance away from you. Settle yourself comfortably and make sure there is plenty of light to work in.

Try out different poses. Do you want to face the mirror, or sit slightly to one side? Do you want to include only your face, or your neck and shoulders as well?

Before you begin your portrait, look closely at your face in the mirror and make sketches of your features. What shape are your eyes? How far apart are they? Is your mouth big or small? Try out different expressions. As you change expression, watch how your eyes, eyebrows, cheeks and mouth move and change shape. By getting to know your face in this way, you will find it easier to draw a good likeness.

Rest your drawing board at an angle so you don't have to move your head too much when you look up from your drawing to the mirror.

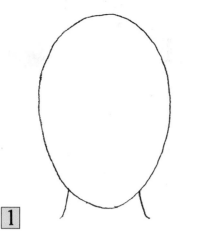

1

Start by drawing an egg shape for the face, and add the neck. Draw very lightly because you might want to make corrections later.

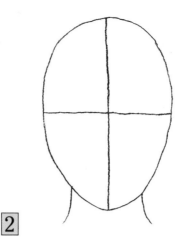

2

Draw a line down the middle of the head. This will help you to position the nose. Draw another line across the middle for the eyes to rest on.

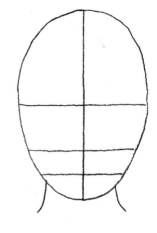

3

Draw a line halfway between the eye line and the chin where the tip of the nose will come. Draw another line between the nose line and the chin. This is where the mouth should go.

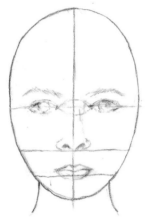

4

Draw rough shapes for the eyes, nose and mouth. Check that they are the right size and in the correct position. On most people, the eyes are about one eye-width apart.

5

Now you can start to fill in the details and draw the hair. Look for the areas of light and shade. First shade in the light areas with light pencil lines.

6

Finally shade in the darkest areas. Don't forget to give your portrait a background.

45

Drawing with pens and markers

Have you tried using felt-tip pens, markers and ball-point pens for drawing? Drawing with pens is good practice because it makes you work boldly – once you have made a mark on the paper it has to stay there. Don't be put off because you can't rub out your mistakes – just go over the lines again. Lines and wrinkles make faces more interesting – and the same goes for drawings!

Pens and markers come in hundreds of colours and a wide choice of nib shapes, from very fine points to chunky, wedge-shaped tips.

Fine points are good for lines and details.

Bullet-shaped points make thicker lines and dots.

Wedge-shaped tips are useful for filling in areas of colour. You can also use the edge of the nib to make fine lines and graduated "italic" curves.

Rolling-ball pens are pleasant to draw with. They give lines of even width.

Ordinary ball-point pens can be used in the same way, but they are not so smooth.

Drawing out and about

Felt-tips and pens are great for outdoor sketching because they are easy to carry around and you can draw very quickly with them. The colours dry quickly, and there are no brushes to clean.

Take a pocket notebook and pen with you when you are out and about. When you spot something interesting, make a quick sketch there and then. Here are some places where you will find plenty of people – and interesting backgrounds – to draw:

- Trains and buses
- A trip to the shops
- The zoo
- The fairground
- The local sports ground
- The beach

Try combining different nib shapes and thicknesses in the same drawing. This picture shows some effects you can achieve with markers and pens.

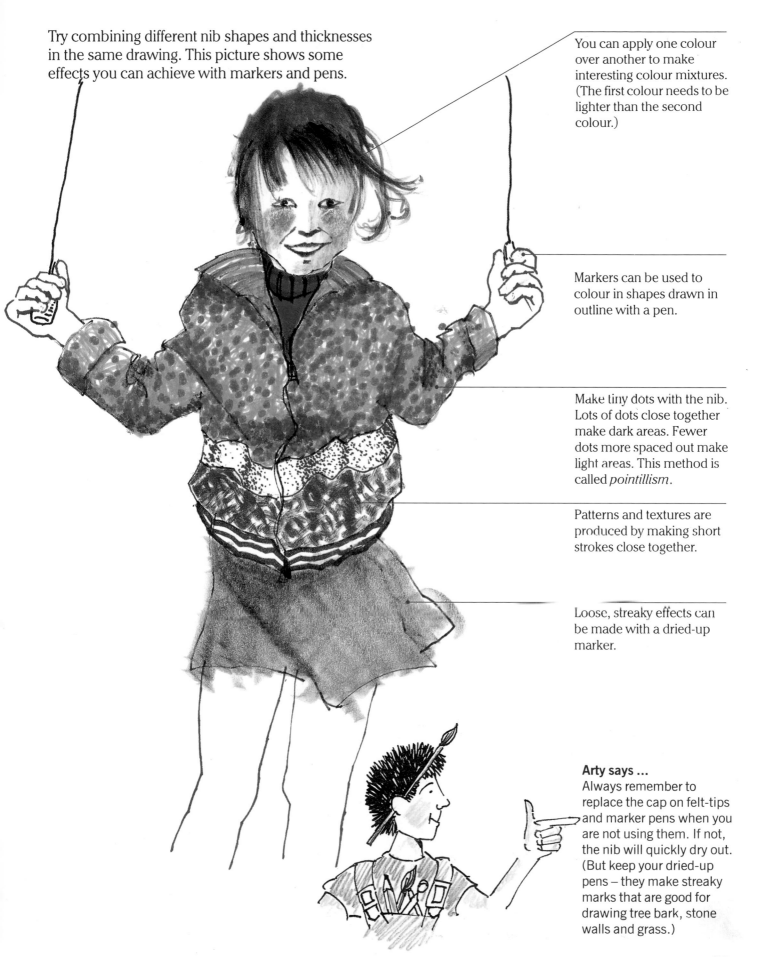

You can apply one colour over another to make interesting colour mixtures. (The first colour needs to be lighter than the second colour.)

Markers can be used to colour in shapes drawn in outline with a pen.

Make tiny dots with the nib. Lots of dots close together make dark areas. Fewer dots more spaced out make light areas. This method is called *pointillism*.

Patterns and textures are produced by making short strokes close together.

Loose, streaky effects can be made with a dried-up marker.

Arty says ...
Always remember to replace the cap on felt-tips and marker pens when you are not using them. If not, the nib will quickly dry out. (But keep your dried-up pens – they make streaky marks that are good for drawing tree bark, stone walls and grass.)

47

Light and shade

O ur bodies are not flat, like a pancake; they are solid and round. But when we paint and draw figures, how can we make them look solid and round on a flat sheet of paper? The answer is by using light and shade. When light hits any object it creates light parts and dark parts. The parts nearest to the light are the brightest. The parts facing away from the light are the darkest. By observing this in your drawings and paintings you can make your figures look more lifelike.

This shape is a circle. On the page opposite, we have changed the circle into a ball, by adding shadows.

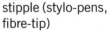

The face on the left looks flat, like a cartoon drawing. By adding shadows, we have made the figure look real and lifelike.

Drawing shadows

Shadows on the figure usually fade gradually from dark to light. Different ways of drawing shadows give different effects. Close or wide spacing on **hatching** or **cross-hatching** gives dark or light areas. Add interest to both with thick and thin lines, lines in different directions, or two or more colours. **Stipple** dots, widely or closely spaced, give light or dark areas. **Smudging** with your finger can evenly blend shadows from light to dark.

hatching (pen and ink, biro, fibre-tip, stylo-pens)

smudging (chalk, crayon soft pencil, charcoal)

cross-hatching (pen and ink, biro, fibre-tip, stylo-pens)

stipple (stylo-pens, fibre-tip)

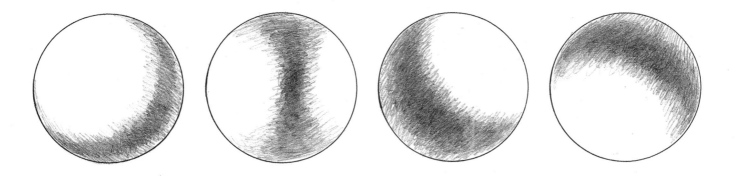

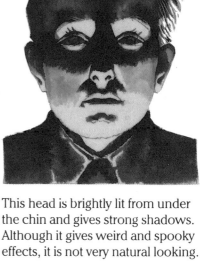

The light on this face comes from the left, just above the head. This sort of lighting is good for a natural sort of portrait with soft shadows.

This head is brightly lit from the side, giving strong contrast to shadows and highlights. This sort of lighting can add lots of drama to a portrait.

This head is brightly lit from under the chin and gives strong shadows. Although it gives weird and spooky effects, it is not very natural looking.

Cast Shadows

The shadows cast by an object onto the ground are important too. Without them your figures look as if they are floating in mid air! The length of a cast shadow depends on the position of the sun in the sky.

When the sun is high in the sky, the shadow is short.

When the sun is low in the sky, the shadow is long.

Remember that shadows always fall in the opposite direction to where the sun is shining from. Look at these two pictures: can you tell where the sun is?

49

Torn-paper pictures

This project is fun to do, and will help you to observe the patterns of light and shade on your subject and to copy them. The idea is to look at the colours in your subject and decide how light or dark they are. For instance, your sweater might be dark red, but in bright sunshine some parts of the sweater will look much lighter than others, because the light shines brightly on some parts and makes dark shadows on other parts.

Arty says...
Try screwing up your eyes when you look at your subject. This makes it easier to see the contrast between light areas and dark areas.

1

Start by collecting sheets of black, white and grey paper. Newspaper is good, or sugar paper. You will also need scissors, glue and a sheet of paper.

2

Find a magazine photo of a face with strong light and dark contrasts.

3

On a large sheet of paper, copy or trace the outline of the face only.

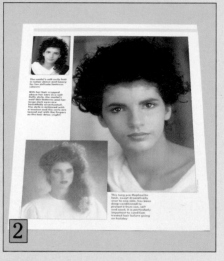

4

Now look for all the light areas and all the dark areas on the face. Copy the shapes of these light and dark areas onto your drawing, as if you were drawing a map or completing a jigsaw.

5 Now decide which are the darkest areas, the lightest areas, and the areas that are in between light and dark. Make a "collage" of the face from torn paper. Take your piece of black paper and tear it into shapes that fit the areas of dark colour on the photograph (they don't have to be exact). Glue the shapes in place.

6 Do the same with torn pieces of white paper, and glue them onto the areas of lightest colour.

7 Finally, do the same with pieces of grey paper, gluing them to the shapes you decided were in between the lightest and the darkest. You should now have a black and white version of the original coloured photograph!

51

Mixing colours

When you decide to paint something, you must look carefully at the subject and try to see all the different colours and shades within it. Then you have to know how to mix the colours you see in it using the paints you have. It is important to learn how paints mix, because it will help make your paintings more realistic. It also saves you money, because from just a few tubes of paint you can make many different shades and tones, simply by mixing different colours together. These pages will show you how to mix paints to get all the colours you need.

A rainbow is made up of seven colours: red, orange, yellow, green, blue, indigo (dark blue) and violet (purple), in that order. All the colours you see around you are made from these colours.

The colour wheel
To make colour mixing easy to understand, artists invented an idea called the colour wheel. The colour wheel is like a rainbow, only made into a circle. The colours are in the same order as they appear in a rainbow. You can make your own colour wheel using watercolour paints (poster paints don't work very well for colour mixing). Draw a circle and divide it into six equal sections. Colour the sections red, orange, yellow, green, blue and violet (purple).

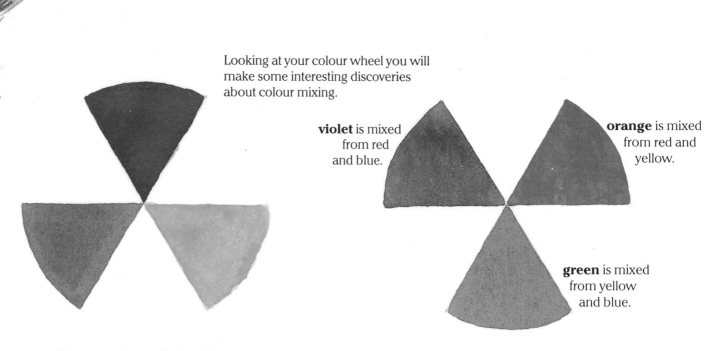

Looking at your colour wheel you will make some interesting discoveries about colour mixing.

violet is mixed from red and blue.

orange is mixed from red and yellow.

green is mixed from yellow and blue.

Primary colours Red, yellow and blue cannot be mixed from other colours. They are called *primary colours*.

Secondary colours These are made by mixing any two primary colours together.

So, starting with the three primary colours – red, yellow and blue – it is possible to mix lots and lots of different colours. Clever, isn't it! And you can make different shades of each colour by adding a little black to darken them, or white to lighten them.

red...

plus white

plus more white

black has been added here

...and even more white

Mixing colours You can increase the colours on your colour wheel to twelve, by mixing together any two colours that lie next to each other on the six-colour wheel. This gives you what are called *tertiary colours* (pronounced "ter-shary"), which are red-orange, yellow-orange, yellow-green, blue-green, blue-violet and red-violet.

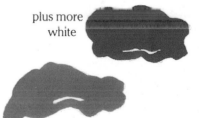

Arty says...
Why not make your own colour card like the ones paint manufacturers produce? Draw small squares on a sheet of paper and fill them in with all the exciting colours you have mixed. Give each colour an appropriate and descriptive name, such as "rebellion red" or "soggy cabbage green".

When you have discovered how to mix colours that are next to each other on the colour wheel, try using colours that are opposite each other on the wheel.

yellow is the complementary colour of violet

blue is the complementary colour of orange

green is the complementary colour of red

When two complementary colours are placed next to each other they look very bright and vibrant. Use complementary colours to make a picture look exciting and energetic.

Complementary colours Colours opposite each other on the colour wheel are called *complementary colours*. Green is the complementary colour of red; blue is the complementary of orange and yellow is the complementary of violet. Notice that each primary colour is always opposite a secondary colour. It is never opposite another primary colour.

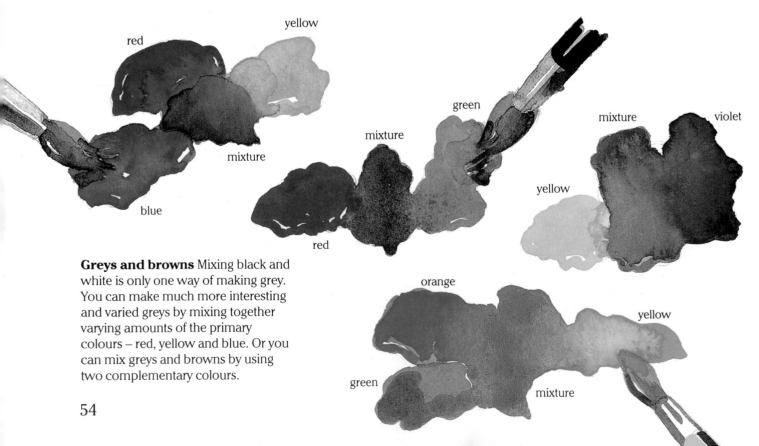

red yellow

mixture

blue

mixture

red

green

mixture

violet

yellow

orange

green

mixture

yellow

Greys and browns Mixing black and white is only one way of making grey. You can make much more interesting and varied greys by mixing together varying amounts of the primary colours – red, yellow and blue. Or you can mix greys and browns by using two complementary colours.

Warm and cool colours

The colour wheel shows that colours can be divided into two types – warm and cool. On one side are the warm colours – the reds, oranges and yellows of fire. On the other side are the cool colours – the blues and greens of grass and water. Warm and cool colours play an important part in paintings. For example, in a portrait the shadows are usually dark and cool, containing greys, blues and greens. The parts of the figure exposed to the light are brighter and warmer in colour.

The paintings on the left and right are by the same artist. However, each one has a very different feel because of the different types of colours used by the artist. The painting of three children on the beach (on the left) is painted mainly in warm yellows and oranges (with splashes of their complementary colours violet and blue) to give the feeling of a hot summer day. The picture on the right, called "It's freezing", *looks* freezing because it was painted mainly in cool blues and blue-greens.

Make a Colour Scrapbook

Keep scraps of coloured paper, fabric and sweet wrappers and make a colour scrapbook. See how many different kinds of each colour you can collect. Label the colours "warm", "cool", "bright", "pale" and so on.

Painting with only a few colours

I t is tempting to use lots of different colours when you paint a picture. But why not challenge yourself sometimes, and paint a picture using just a few colours? It's a good way to learn about colours and what happens to them when you mix them together.

If you've read page 53 you will know that it is possible to create a wide range of colours by mixing the three primary colours – red, yellow and blue – to make secondary and tertiary colours. As a project, try painting a portrait or figure using just three colours plus white. The portrait on the opposite page was painted this way, and it is very lifelike.

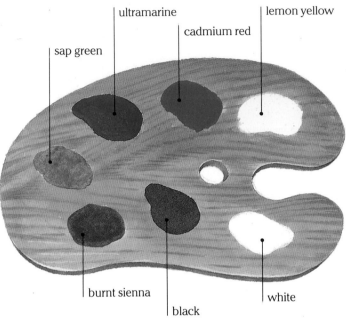

sap green
ultramarine
cadmium red
lemon yellow
burnt sienna
black
white

Arty says...
Use a piece of scrap paper to test colours before putting them on your painting. You can test your colour mixing skills by trying to mix a colour to match a coloured piece of paper.

Instead of spending your money on dozens of tubes of cheap paint, buy five or six tubes of good-quality paint in useful colours – you will get far better results. Here is a list of recommended colours:

- Lemon yellow
- Cadmium red
- Ultramarine (a warm blue)
- Sap green
- Burnt sienna (a warm brown)
- Black
- White

Painting with one colour

See if you can make a painting using only one colour. Choose any colour you like, and mix three different shades of it in separate dishes. Make a dark, a light and a medium shade.

For the dark shade, mix the colour with a little black. For the light shade, mix the colour with a little white. For the medium shade, mix the colour with just a little water. Use your colour to paint the light, dark and medium areas in your subject.

As you can see, painting with only one colour can be very effective. It gives a strong impression of light and shade.

These are the colours the artist started off with:

These are the colours that were mixed from the original colours. Some colours were mixed with white to make them lighter. Some colours were mixed with black to make them darker.

Painting skin

What colour is skin? We might say that skin is "brown" or "white" or "pink" or "black". But when we look closely, we can see all sorts of colours in our skin – including grey, green and blue! This is because skin reflects the colours around it. Test this for yourself by looking at the back of your hand in bright sunlight and then in shadow – see how the colour of your skin appears to change? Look especially at the shadowy parts – do they sometimes look bluish or greenish? Next time you paint people, think about how you can mix your colours to make the skin look more realistic. These pages give you some tips.

1

Arty says…
Mix up some paint and see if you can match it to your own skin colour. Test your mixture by dabbing some paint onto the back of your hand to see how closely it matches. Below are some blobs of paint of different skin colours.

Look for the light and dark parts of the skin – the highlights and shadows – and mix light and dark colours for each. This is how artists make their figures look real, as if we could reach out and touch them. Usually the parts that stick out, like the nose and forehead, are lighter, and the parts that go in, like the hollow under the bottom lip, are darker.

1 For this portrait, the artist first of all filled in the main areas of shadow, using blocks of dark colour. The picture has been painted on coloured paper, rather than white, which gives an interesting effect.
2 Next, some details were painted in and more highlights added with white paint.

58

3 On the finished picture, the shadows have been blended and the edges softened. Parts of the paper have been left to show through on some of the lighter parts of the face.

Right and wrong

☒ If you add black to make skin darker in the shadow parts, the colour looks muddy and dead.

☑ Instead, try adding a small touch of brown, blue or green to the basic skin colour for the shadow parts. You'll find it looks more realistic.

Skin colour

Some people have very light skin, some have very dark skin, and others are somewhere in between. Here are three portraits of people from different ethnic backgrounds – see how the artist has used different colour mixtures to paint each one.

Mixtures of brown, grey, blue and violet were used for this portrait. Black was used for the hair – but not for the skin.

This girl has pale skin. The artist used yellow, pink and brown, and left some areas white, to model the shape of her face.

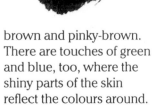

This man might be Asian or Latin American. His skin is a dark, warm brown. Notice how the artist has modelled the face with patches of dark brown, orangey-brown and pinky-brown. There are touches of green and blue, too, where the shiny parts of the skin reflect the colours around.

61

Hair

When you are drawing hair it is not a good idea to try to draw the separate strands. This makes your subjects look as if they have spaghetti sprouting out of their heads! For a better effect, start by drawing the outline shape of the hair, then make a few lines and strokes in the same direction as the hair grows. Short curls can be drawn with groups of C-shaped strokes. Draw wavy hair with S-shaped strokes.

Notice the areas of light and shade on the hair (screw up your eyes to see them better). The top of the hair is usually lighter, because light shines on it from above. The hair on one side of the head may be lighter if it faces the direction of the light.

If you are painting shiny hair, try leaving small areas of the white paper unpainted to show the highlights (see the girl in the blue sweater at the bottom of the next page).

Always use light, feathery strokes with your pencil or brush. If you press too hard the hair will look solid and hard instead of soft.

These pictures show step-by-step how to paint hair seen from the front and from the side.

Paint the head first. Make sure you get the proportions right. Then paint the outline of the hair.

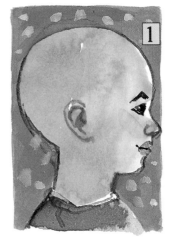

Hair comes in many different styles – long and short, straight and curly, wavy and spiky. People's hairstyles help us to identify who they are. Men sometimes have beards, moustaches and bushy eyebrows, too. Here are some examples of different hairstyles – see how many you can spot next time you are out and about.

There are several different methods you can use to express the texture of hair. Some of these are shown below.

Let the paint dry. Finally, add a few thin strokes with the tip of your brush.

While the paint is still damp, scratch into it with the end of your brush to indicate a few strands here and there.

Wipe most of the paint off your brush then skim the brush lightly over the paper. This makes feathery, broken strokes that look like strands of hair.

Apply a thin wash of colour. When it is dry, make light strokes over it with coloured pencils.

Strokes of pastel or charcoal can be softly blended together with your finger.

With watercolour paint you can paint one wash of colour over another while the first is still damp. The colours mix together to create a soft effect.

Apply strokes of wax crayon and then scratch out some lines with a sharp point to indicate a few strands.

How to draw and paint clothes

When you draw and paint people, pay special attention to the clothes they are wearing. Clothes usually follow the shape of the body, so if you draw them correctly they can help you to make the figure look rounded instead of flat. For example, the collar of a shirt follows the round shape of the neck, the sleeves of a dress wrap around the arms, the tops of socks wrap around the legs, and a belt wraps around the waist.

Look at the patterns on clothing, too. The lines of stripes and checks are not always straight – they bend where they wrap around arms and legs.

The folds and creases in clothes indicate how the body is moving. In this picture of a skipping girl, see how the folds in her dress give a feeling of the skirt swinging as she jumps up and down.

Costumes Ask your friends to dress up in costume and pose for you while you paint them.

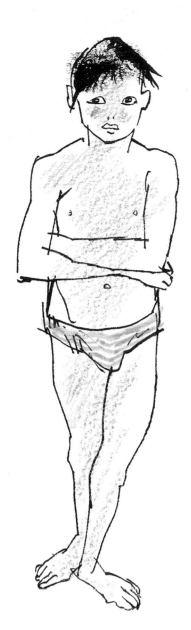

Putting on clothes

Look at the way the clothes have been drawn in this picture.

The hat band and brim follow the round shape of the head.

The collar follows the round shape of the neck.

The jacket sleeves crease up at the bend of the elbow.

Don't forget details such as buttons, pocket flaps and so on to make your drawing realistic.

Note how the pattern of the trousers follows the rounded forms of the legs.

Prints and patterns

Collect scraps of fabric in different patterns and colours. See how many patterns you can find – checks, stripes, flowers, spots and dots and so on. Draw squares on a sheet of paper and fill them in with your patterns – like these ones here.

In the 18th century rich men and women wore very elaborate clothes made from fine materials such as silk, satin and lace. This portrait is of a French lady, Madame de Pompadour. Why not make a copy of this painting, or collect pieces of paper or fabric and make a collage?

These pictures show, step by step, how to paint the folds in clothes.

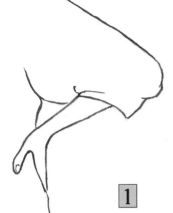 **1**

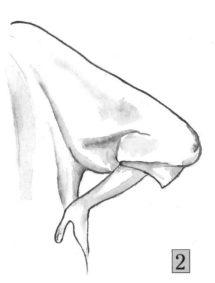 **2**

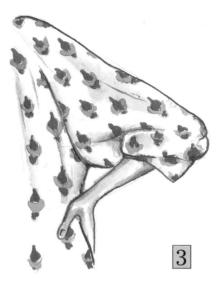 **3**

1 Draw the outline.

2 Draw the biggest folds and paint the shadows (don't make them too dark).

3 When the paint is dry add the pattern of the fabric. See how the folds make the patterns stretch and bend.

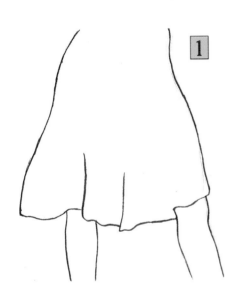 **1**

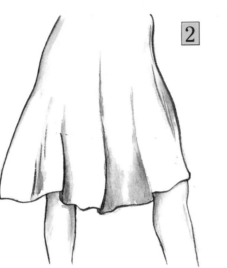 **2**

 **3**

These close-ups, taken from the portrait on the opposite page, show how the artist has carefully painted Madame de Pompadour's clothes. The fabric of the skirt looks smooth and shiny.

The stripes follow the form of the bow.

There are lots of folds in the lace of her sleeve.

In this close-up, see how the light and shade on the sleeve shows the roundness of her arm.

67

Using paints

There are lots of different kinds of paint to choose from in the shops. Some come in bottles, some in tins, some in tubes. It is worth buying good-quality paints as they last longer and the colours are stronger.

Powder paints are cheap to buy, but you have to mix them with water before you can use them. Put some powder into a dish or jar and add the water a little at a time. The paint should be thick and creamy. If it is too runny your paintings will look dull and wishy-washy.

Poster paints come in jars. They are runny, but quite thick. Poster paints are brightly coloured and they are more shiny than powder paints.

Watercolour paints come in small blocks. You wet your brush with water and rub it over the block to pick up the paint. Watercolour paint is much thinner and runnier than powder paints and poster paints. Always use white paper with watercolour paints.

Experiment with your paints to see what you can do with them. As well as mixing colours together on a palette, you can mix them on the paper by letting two colours run together while they are wet. Try impressing objects such as sponges, leaves or bits of rough cloth into the wet paint to create textures.

Always replace the lids on your paints when you have finished, so they don't dry out. And always wash your brushes after you have used them, otherwise the paint will clog up the hairs. Store your brushes with the bristles upwards in an empty pot or jar.

With thin paint and the tip of a small brush, you can "draw" lines.

This interesting colour mixture was made by letting three different colours run into each other while still wet.

To show light and shadow on objects, first paint the light parts. Mix the paint with plenty of water. When the paint is dry, paint the shadow parts with a darker shade, made by using more paint and less water.

Paint like the Impressionists!

On page 53 we described how to mix two colours together to make a third colour. Here is another way of colour "mixing", called broken colour. Instead of mixing two colours together with a brush, you apply separate strokes or dabs of one colour, leaving spaces between them. Then you fill in the spaces with the other colour. It's a bit like making a mosaic. From a distance, the two colours seem to merge together and make a third colour. For example, you can make green from dabs, spots or strokes of blue and yellow.

The French Impressionist painters used broken colour all the time because it gives a more interesting effect than flat, mixed colour.

Dots, dabs and dribbles of colour were used to make this picture of a woman sewing. Colours applied in this way appear very lively and vibrant.

Start by making strokes with your first colour. Leave spaces between the strokes.

When the first colour is dry, fill in the spaces with your second colour. Always wash your brush between colours. You can let the strokes overlap if you like.

You can apply your colours in lots of different ways. Try making tiny dots like these...

... or big, bold slabs of colour.

Broken colour works well with felt-tip pens, crayons and pastels, too. Try making a "broken colour" picture using these different techniques.

This portrait was painted in 1905 by a French artist, André Derain. It is of his friend Henri Matisse, who was also an artist. Derain painted the face with big blocks of colour, like a mosaic. See how he used warm yellows and reds on one side of the face, where the light hits it. On the other side he used cool blues, where the face is in shadow. Using thick poster paints or wax crayons, try making a copy of Derain's portrait.

Spitting images

When you draw or paint someone's portrait, your aim is to make your picture look as much like that person as possible. If you do a portrait of your friend Tim, and your other friends say "wow, that's the spitting image of Tim!" you can feel very proud of yourself, because getting a good likeness of someone is not easy!

So what is the secret? Before you begin drawing, take a good long look at your model. What do you notice first about him or her? Is it the hair, the eyes or the mouth? How long is the hair, and exactly what colour is it? Is the face long and thin, or is it round? Are the eyes large or small? What shape is the nose? Is the mouth wide, or small and button-like? Does your model have freckles? These are the kinds of questions you should ask yourself; look at each individual feature carefully before you draw it.

You might like to start by drawing the shape of the face first. Or you might prefer to draw the eyes, nose and mouth and then draw the face around it. Keep looking back at your model while you draw, and keep checking all the time that you have got the shapes right and the features in the correct position.

Below are paintings of six different children. What are the most noticeable features of each one? (Answers below each picture.)

Blond curly hair, dark eyes and freckles. Wearing a green polo-necked sweater.

Dark hair, blue eyes and a red nose. Wearing a red scarf, tied cowboy-style.

Black curly hair and freckled red cheeks. Wearing blue-rimmed spectacles and a shirt and tie.

Things like jewellery and hats can help to make your portraits look more interesting.

Two schoolfriends made drawings of each other in class. On the left is a portrait of Emma, drawn by Alexandra aged 10. On the right is a portrait of Alexandra, drawn by Emma, also aged 10.

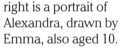
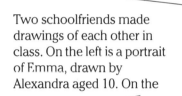

Dark hair tied in pigtails with blue bows, and a freckled nose. Wearing gold earrings and a dress with a collar.

Dark curly hair, heavy eyebrows and bright blue eyes. Wearing a dress with a frilly collar.

Long red hair and lots of freckles. Wearing red beads and a red Alice band.

What is a portrait?

A portrait is a very special kind of painting. A really good portrait not only looks like the person being painted, it also tells us something about what kind of person they are, what kind of clothes they like to wear, and what their interests are. A portrait tells a story about the person you are painting – a story told in one picture, without words.

Try painting a portrait of someone you know well. Look at your model and ask yourself "what is it that makes this person special? How can I show this in my painting?" Think about how you can include objects in the picture that tell us something about the person and make the picture more interesting. For instance, if you are painting your mum, and she likes gardening, why not paint a portrait of her in the garden, surrounded by her favourite flowers?

Finnian Brigham, aged 10

Heather Sygrove, aged 11

Family portraits

These "family portraits" are all very different. Try and guess what sort of personalities these people might have. Then make a portrait of your family or friends. Try and think about expression and "body language" (see pages 34 and 35), as well as including objects which tell us more about the people in the picture.

Emma Appleby, aged 9

74

The portrait shown here was painted by an artist called Jan Van Eyck in the 15th century. It is called "The Arnolfini Marriage" and depicts an Italian merchant and his bride. The picture shows the marriage actually taking place in their own home.

The scene is reflected in the mirror on the back wall. We can also see two other people who have entered the room.

The single candle in the chandelier is a marriage candle.

The couple are holding hands.

The groom's hand is raised as he swears a solemn oath.

The dog is a griffin terrier, which was a symbol of loyalty in olden times.

Making a collage

Collage is an exciting way of making pictures. Instead of using paints or crayons, you cut shapes out of scraps of paper and cloth and small objects and glue them to the paper. It's a bit like doing a jigsaw, only you make the shapes yourself. You can stick the shapes on top of each other as well as next to each other.

Famous artists like Pablo Picasso have made collage pictures. It's great fun to find odd bits of scrap material and to use your imagination to put them together to make a picture full of exciting colours, shapes and textures. (By *texture* we mean what things feel like. Custard has a smooth texture, porridge has a knobbly texture; cloth has a soft texture, wood has a hard texture, and so on.)

For this portrait Nichola, aged 10, used small squares of coloured paper which she had cut from a magazine. The effect is rather like a Roman mosaic.

Mark, aged 9, used only two kinds of material – wool and nylon – for his collage. But it works very well because he's layered the net to give a nice texture. Tim drew the profile first in pencil.

This picture (by Emma, aged 7) also uses wool for hair, but this time fabric has been used for the face. Look at how she's painted on the rosy cheeks. Using paint as well as 'bits and pieces' in a collage can give really interesting effects.

76

All sorts of materials can be used to make a collage. Why not make a 'collage collection' of odd bits and pieces from around the house – fabric strips, wrapping paper, bits of string and wool, buttons, corrugated cardboard, pebbles, shells, leaves – in fact, anything that has an interesting colour or texture.

You will also need scissors to cut up your collage material, glue to stick them to the paper, sheets of newspaper to protect the table and plenty of rags or tissues to mop up any spills.

Get your balance

The human body has two sides to it. When you make a movement on one side, the other side moves in a different direction in order to keep the body balanced. Stand in front of a mirror and shift your weight onto your right foot. Can you see – and feel – how your left leg bends at the knee, your right hip moves up and your left hip moves down? When you draw people, be aware of how the limbs balance each other in different positions. This will help to make your figure drawings more lifelike.

These skeleton pictures show how our bones and joints move as we bend and stretch.

Moving targets

Find pictures of moving people in books, magazines and newspapers. Stand in front of a long mirror and copy their positions. Try to feel how your body shifts its weight as you move into the position. Make "stick man" drawings of the figures.

78

These sketches show how the body balances itself when it performs different actions. Notice how the body leans away from heavy objects it is pulling or carrying.

Planning your picture

When you paint a picture, think carefully about the people and objects you want to include and where you will place them. Arranging the parts of a picture is called "composition", and a good composition makes a good picture!

Different shapes and sizes add interest and variety to a picture. Overlapping objects and figures will lead the viewer's eye easily from one part to the next. This helps hold the picture together instead of having bits here and there that don't seem to have anything to do with each other. It's best to make some rough sketches first to see which composition works best.

If you want to paint a park scene, for example, think who would bring it to life – you could include a man snoozing in a deckchair, his head covered by a paper, boys playing cricket, a dog chasing a ball, and a gardener mowing the grass.

Compose your own picture

These figures of boys and girls have been drawn to the scale they would appear if they were positioned in the foreground, the middle ground or the background of a picture. Trace out the figures and use them to make up your own compositions. Try making pictures with overlapping figures and compare them with compositions where the figures have lots of space around them. Two examples have already been done in the boxes.

In this picture all of the figures are standing in a straight line and are all the same size (scale).

In this picture the figures are overlapping. Smaller and larger (middle ground and background) figures have been used, giving the picture a feeling of depth.

Look at the different composition of these pictures. You don't always have to place your model in the centre. Experiment by putting him or her at one side of the picture, or by overlapping different people or objects. Using a diagonal composition can help give a sense of movement, as in the picture of the ballet dancers below.

All about scale

Scale means how big or small an object looks when we compare it to another object. For example, a cat is bigger than a mouse, but a cat is much smaller than an elephant!

The odd thing is that when you have two objects of the same size, one close to you and the other far away, the closer object looks much bigger than the one far away. Look at this picture of people sitting in a cinema. The two older people in the **foreground** are painted with much bigger heads than the three people behind in the **middle ground** while the two people furthest away in the **background** have even smaller heads. Painting people different sizes, according to how far away they are, will give your picture the illusion of depth and make it much more interesting to look at.

81

Finger painting

F inger painting is great fun because you can use your fingers – or even your hand – as a paintbrush! These pictures show just some of the exciting patterns and marks you can make with your fingers, thumbs and hands. See if you can think of some more. Then think about how you can combine different marks to make a finger painting of a figure, or a group of figures. Start by making a few trial prints on scrap paper before working on your picture.

Arty says ...
Finger painting works best if the paint is quite thick. Mix a little wallpaper paste into the paint to thicken it.

For finger painting you will need:

- A sheet of paper
- Newspaper
- Poster paints
- A shallow dish to hold the paint
- Plenty of rags for cleaning your fingers
- Felt-tip pens for adding details to your picture

Make long, squiggly lines by dragging your fingers down the paper.

Make tiny dots and spots by pressing very lightly on the paper.

Press the whole of your forefinger into the paint, then press your finger onto the paper to make sausage shapes like these.

Press the edge of your hand into the paint and drag it across the paper.

82

These shapes are made with the fingertips.

Crowd scenes

Here's a great idea for painting a crowd of people. Mix up two or three dishes of paint in different shades of pink and brown. Dip the tip of your forefinger into the paint and press it onto the paper lots of times to make the face shapes. When the paint is dry, use crayons or felt-tips to add hair and features. Add on things like hats, scarves and glasses, too. Here are some places where crowds gather:

- A football match
- A pop concert
- A busy shopping street
- The theatre or cinema
- A carnival

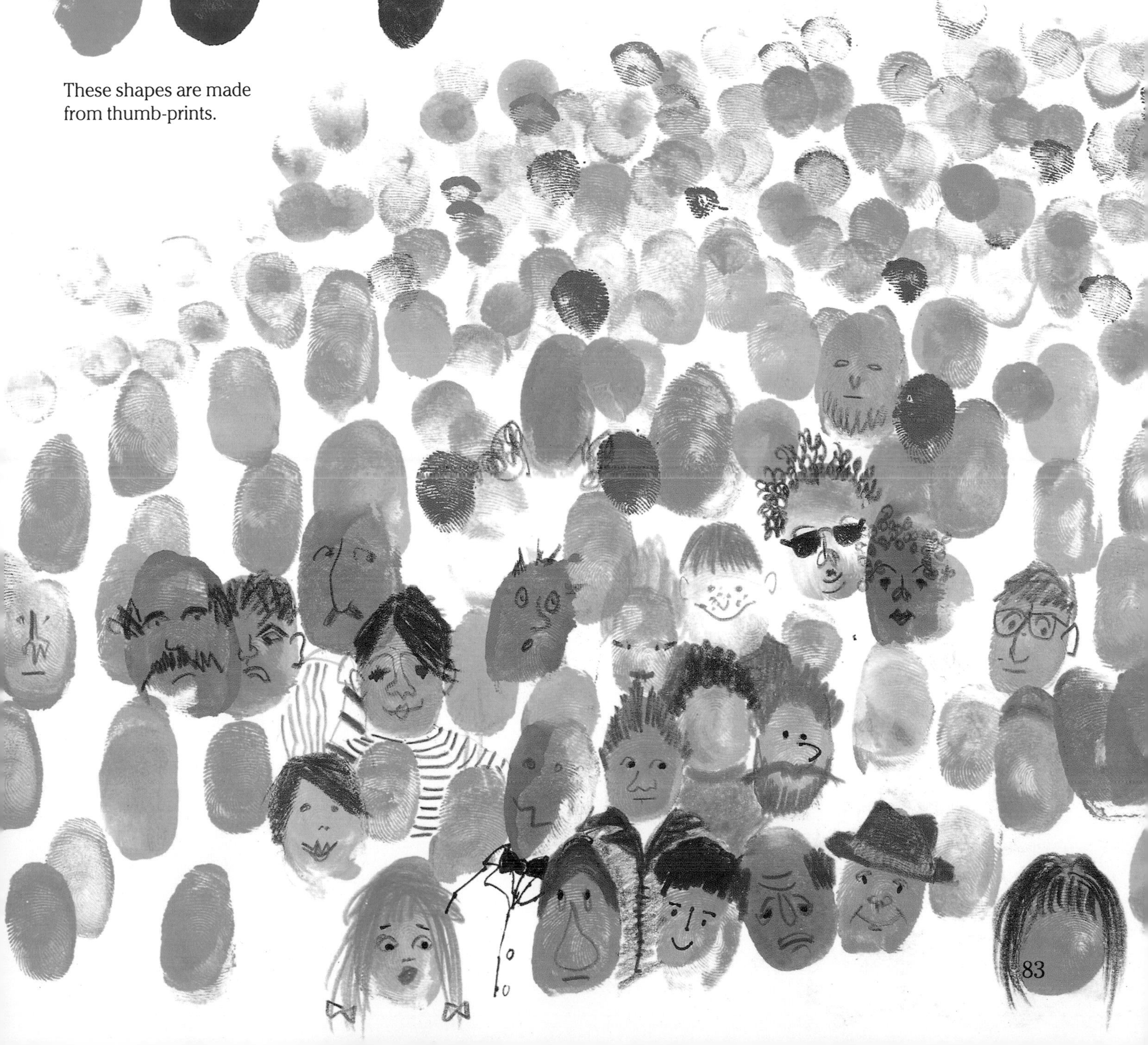

These shapes are made from thumb-prints.

83

Making potato prints

You can make exciting designs and shapes with a potato and some poster paint. Each potato can be cut into two or more pieces to make different designs that can be printed many times. Use potato prints to make repeat patterns for decorating book covers and greeting cards – or use them to make portraits of people or to illustrate a story. When the prints are dry, you can draw more details on them with wax crayons or felt-tip pens.

To make potato prints you will need:
- A raw potato
- Dishes of poster paint
- A sharp knife
- Paper to print onto
- A paint brush
- Crayons or felt-tip pens

Arty says...

Sharp knives can be dangerous, so use them with care. Hold the potato firmly and keep your fingers away from the knife blade in case it slips. When you cut out the potato shape, cut away from you, not towards you. Best of all, get an adult to help you.

Potato-cut cartoons

Invent your own cartoon characters using potato prints. Make simple potato-print face shapes like these. Then, when the paint is dry, use a felt-tip pen to draw amusing features onto the face shapes.

How to make a potato print

Choose a medium-sized potato and cut it in half. Use a felt-tip pen to draw your design on the cut end of one half of the potato; or draw the shape on some paper, cut it out, place it on the potato and trace around it.

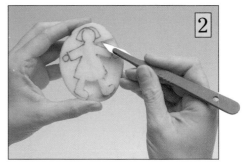

With a sharp knife, carefully cut away the potato around the outside of the shape so that it stands out on its own.

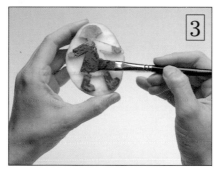

Brush the raised shape with paint. Be careful not to use too much paint, or the finished print will be messy and the colours will run into each other.

Press the potato firmly onto the surface of your paper. You should be able to make two or three prints before applying more paint.

Family and friends

This painting is called *The Luncheon of the Boating Party*. It was painted in 1881 by Pierre Auguste Renoir, one of the French Impressionist painters. The painting is of a group of people enjoying lunch outdoors on a sunny afternoon. The people in the picture are friends of Renoir. The girl with the dog on the left of the picture is Aline Charigot, who later became Renoir's wife.

The picture has a relaxed, happy feel to it. Can you suggest some ways in which the artist expressed this in his painting? There are some suggestions at the bottom of this page.

Study Renoir's painting and then make your own modern-day version of it. You could paint a scene from a celebration, such as a birthday party or a wedding reception. Or perhaps a family picnic or barbeque. You can paint your picture from real life, from imagination, or using a family snapshot as reference.

The people all have their heads turned towards each other. Some have their arms around each other.

Renoir has used warm, sunny colours in the painting to express a happy mood. There are touches of red and yellow all over the painting.

The expressions on the
faces of the people are
relaxed and we can tell they
are chatting happily.

Copying a work of art

Many of the great artists learned to draw and paint by copying the paintings of artists who had gone before. Copying is a good way to learn because it is like stepping into the artist's shoes. As you copy, almost without thinking you discover the way the artist used lines, shapes and colours. Then you can use what you have discovered in your own paintings and drawings.

Visit art galleries, or look at pictures of portraits in books. Choose one you really like and make your own copy of it. Try to find out about the artist. What materials and methods did he or she use? Why was the portrait painted? Who was the portrait of?

This is a portrait of the English writer Somerset Maugham. It was painted in 1949 by Graham Sutherland, an English artist. Somerset Maugham loved the Far East, and lived there for a long time. There are touches of the Far East in the painting. Can you spot them? There is a bamboo stool, and you can just see some palm fronds above Mr Maugham's head.

The background is orange, like the robes of a Buddhist monk. Also notice the way Mr Maugham is sitting and the expression on his face. He looks very aloof and inscrutable, like a wise old man from China. So you see, this portrait is not just a picture of a man. It also tells us something about the man's character and his interests.

Try making a copy of this portrait. The pictures here show copies made by four different children.

Sarah Little, aged 9½

Rhys Wilson, aged 10

Heather Sygrove, aged 11

Finnian Brigham, aged 10

89